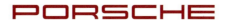

PORSCHE
Cayman
Thrill of the Chase

AUTHORS JUTTA DEISS • ELMAR BRÜMMER • REINER SCHLOZ   **PHOTOGRAPHERS** MARKUS LESER • STEFAN WARTER • INGO BARENSCHEE

MOTORBOOKS

CONTENTS

Introduction
The Hunter and the Hunted — 14

01 Design — 18
INSTINCTIVE AWARENESS
On the Right Track

02 Body — 50
POACHERS AT LARGE
Pack Leader

03 Engine — 60
DID YOU HEAR THAT?
Listening Post
The Hunt is On

04 Road Dynamics — 74
FOLLOWING THE TRAIL
On the Scent
On the Trail of Driving Pleasure
An Agile Lightweight

05 Experience — 96
WILD AND FREE
Where Danger Threatens
Tracing Tradition

06 Communication — 132
THE HUNTING INSTINCT
This Way!

Technical Data — 144

THE CAYMAN is a member of the alligator family; it can be up to 180 centimeters long, and is spoken of as the 'baby crocodile'. Not the friendliest of babies!

THE NORTHERN PART OF SOUTH AMERICA as far down as Uruguay – this is the cayman's hunting ground. It makes jungle rivers, swamps and ponds there rather hazardous.

THIS CAYMAN is a thoroughbred sports car and a member of the Porsche family. It uses a mid-engine concept like the Boxster, but is a model with its own well-defined character.

NEW YORK or Berlin, mountain passes or fast German 'autobahns' – the Cayman adapts brilliantly to its environment worldwide, wherever its tires can grip an asphalt road.

THE CAYMAN is a hunter with a healthy appetite, especially if the menu includes insects, clams, molluscs, amphibians and fish.

THIS BABY CROCODILE earns our respect by its aggressive behavior and sharp teeth. Mother nature helps: the cayman is agile, tough and belligerent. Careful: it bites!

THIS CAYMAN hunts happily for maximum driving pleasure, and motivates drivers who appreciate this and use the gas pedal accordingly.

A MID-ENGINE COUPE of fascinating, sporty character: Porsche's technical people have seen to that. The Cayman is agile and powerful: Beware, it too could bite!

THE HUNTER AND THE HUNTED

Developing a mid-engine coupé to take its place between Boxster and 911 Carrera seems to have aroused the Porsche engineers' hunting instinct: the Cayman is their trophy.

Is it just a deception tactic, the way it stands so firmly on its broad wheels and tires? If so, it's a fascinating one – a Porsche specialty elegantly interpreted on yet another fine new model. It seems to say: I'm perfect, want me! This perfection continues of course under the skin, though all the work that went into it can't be seen. The Cayman crouches as if to say 'Flattery will get you everywhere!', and flexes its back muscles ready to spring, ready to take on the world.

On a glorious day not so very long ago, the automobile engineers in Weissach decided to search for a new car. The trail led them along a path between the recent Boxster and the company's well-established classic, the 911. In other words to drivers who had caught the 'Boxster bug' and wished to experience the next-higher level of Porsche fascination without moving on to a 911 model.

A tempting challenge for creative engineers. The original concept was to give the Boxster, a car conceived as a pure roadster, a more powerful engine and a coupé body. Most cars develop differently: first the coupé, then the convertible. But ambitious hunters don't give up just because the first trail they follow happens to end in a swamp ... to put it bluntly, a pepped-up Boxster wasn't enough to satisfy Porsche's experts. After a brief pause for thought, the fascinating basic idea was revived: a mid-engine coupé with its own special sporty handling. The hunting season was on again, this time with the Boxster acting only as the starting point. New, convincing but rather immodest development targets were drawn up. What was the intended booty this time? A new sports car with its own individual looks and bold night-time design, retaining all the typical features of a Porsche. A pure two-seater, with optimized interior ergonomics that would surround the occupants with a special sense of space. An engine compartment integrated elegantly into the rear trunk. Dynamic performance, efficient aerodynamics, massive braking power and active safety allied to maximum comfort and convenience – in other words top value in all the areas expected of a Porsche.

A wild animal waiting to be tracked down and tamed and a typical Porsche sports car: the Cayman. With an agile 3.4-liter flat six engine delivering 295 bhp (217 kW). An exceptionally sporty 'feel-good car'. Such a successful concept that the most noble of titles simply had to be bestowed on it from the very start: this Cayman is in fact a Cayman S.

There are aspects of quality that one can sense as soon as one gets behind the wheel. Others, on the other hand, depend on concealed technical finesse and the use of high-grade materials. They include the spectacular methods that were found for the production of complex body elements that the stylists and body experts had fought hard to have adopted. Then there were the acoustics experts, who composed a potent melody in sound for the Cayman to play. This is no easy matter in a coupé with the engine effectively inside the car. Last but not least, the suspension wizards had their say, and it's well known that at Porsche only the best is good enough for them!

After this no-holds-barred hunting season on the part of the engineers, designers and stylists, what remains? The answer is ultimate driving pleasure. But it can be interesting to learn how it was arrived at; these are tales that deserve to be told, and we are confident that you too will enjoy following the hunt. Take care: the hunted has now become the hunter! ‹

A FINE FIGURE: The Cayman S conceals its technical refinement under a muscular exterior

INSTINCTIVE AWARENESS

01 Design

ON THE RIGHT TRACK

One idea chases another. On the designers' home ground, instinct leads to success. The way the new Cayman S looks tells you that the hunt is on!

It's just a feeling, we sometimes say. But why "just"? Feelings are an essential element in our lives, and play their part in sports car design too. Always assuming that the feelings are genuine. Which brings us to the next difficult question: how can we develop strong feelings about an object that doesn't yet exist? Pinky Lai, the designer mainly responsible for the Cayman, and his colleagues at the Design Studio in Weissach, start every new project with a big question mark. As Lai puts it: "We have to look for that extra something, the emotional factor." Dreams have a power that can be sensed. Yet common sense is deliberately ignored at the start: "We avoid the direct route from A to B and explore other directions first." Dreams need room to develop and take shape. Detours and diversions, reversals and risks are all permissible as long as one doesn't completely lose sight of the target. The destination input to the 'creative navigation system' was formulated as follows: "To realize a new car concept, but for the Cayman to be immediately identifiable as an authentic Porsche and to set itself apart from the Boxster and the 911 Carrera."

Once the trail has been laid, the designers begin to imagine where it could take them. The first step from notion to idea is 'brainstorming'. Designers have an invaluable advantage over other forward-thinking groups: the energy generated by their brains is converted more rapidly into actual physical form. Their flashes of inspiration can be communicated immediately on paper. In this case the flashes amounted to a full-scale electrical storm. Why can't the Cayman be muzzled? The answer is to be sought in the design freedom that created it. Compact, efficient, ingenious – these fixed elements of its personality could be joined together to produce a variety of silhouettes. Pinky Lai's laptop still contains a collection of initial sketches. As he runs through them by mouse-click, his gaze lingers on the screen – the visionary reviewing the material that inspired the finished product.

The profile of the new Porsche took shape rapidly in the concept phase. Various outlines crystallized into the special sweep of the body that was later to be a dominant feature of the Cayman. Some of the sketches are wild, some are mild, but before long the compact basic shape can be seen to emerge. It's surprising how little 'drama' goes into the creation of a 'dramatic' new model. The two-seater coupé gradually acquires its final form, but even in the detailing phase the designers continue to explore the limits of their package. Pinky Lai: "Freedom of thought is essential. Fantasy has to be kept on the move so that it can generate emotion." But at this stage, emotion is confronted by two practicable alternatives, each full of promise. By now the designers are working on the drafts with the aid of special digital software. In a decision-taking process known as an 'audition', the version with a greater sense of length is chosen. According to a old rule of thumb: when in doubt, add length! The basic design has been found, though it will surely be varied, optimized, examined and refined many times over.

The Cayman now begins to acquire its contours, a unique style appropriate to its concept. For its creators, the Cayman is "emotionally charged" in the most positive of senses. Pinky Lai prefers to speak of "sculptures taking shape"– sculptures on wheels in this particular case. Like the great sculptors of the past, the sports car designers practise a style of their own, yet are never content merely to duplicate an earlier work of art. »

IMAGINATIVE POWER: The first sketches are a mirror of the designer's soul

01 Design

"Even the purist character of the Porsche brand is open to further development, with an end-product that lies somewhere between art and everyday life." The decisive factor is for beauty to be sensual rather than sentimental. "A Porsched must have substance and content in every area, both technical and stylistic." This explains the Cayman's avoidance of compromise down to the smallest design detail.

True art, as we have seen in so many cases, involves satisfying diametrically opposed needs. To insist on bold effects for their own sake is not enough for the sensitive artist. And to subject one's ideas to passing fashion in times of rapid change would be even more hazardous. The Cayman's outlines can be defined as a 'style-forming measure', a claim of some standing that implies a certain timeless character in sports car design. There have been plenty of examples of this in the Porsche company's history. Close links with this tradition mean that modern design at Porsche will never degenerate into flirtation with superficial styling features. The Cayman, the latest asset in the Porsche model program, has no intention of denying its fundamental family relationship. Pinky Lai confirms this: "We made sure that the Cayman harmonizes with the Boxster family." Dynamics with an obvious origin. And they won't go out of date overnight.

What does the designer's art consist of? The answer is surely a blend of creation and seduction. Love of the automobile differs only to a slight degree from other forms of affection in our lives. To allow oneself to be seduced is a subtle, intelligent undertaking. The consequences of the art of seduction were evident when the Cayman was finished and shown in all its glory to dealers and important customers. The Porsche company uses the term "turnaround" for its successful economic recovery in the nineteen-nineties. Now we need a new term such as "head-turner" or maybe "neck-twister" for the reaction provoked by the new Cayman. Pinky Lai grins: "As it was driven past, they simply had to turn their heads for a second look! At moments like these we can tell that our efforts have been successful."

The Cayman is genuine eye candy. From the powerful initial vision, a silhouette has developed that signals pure attack, pure forward thrust. The new coupé front end is emphasized by the slightly oval headlamps and the three boldly shaped air inlets. The foglamps, integrated into the outer air inlets and secured to horizontal bars, and the marker lights emphasize Porsche's current policy of installing separate front lighting elements. Would it be too far-fetched to interpret this after-dark light pattern as a visual link with the cayman, the baby crocodile itself? Creative people accept such comparisons as an indirect compliment for their stylistic talent as designers – a difficult task at the best of times. The large front air inlets are of course needed to satisfy the demands of a powerful engine and an effective brake system. To exhibit true style in the face of such constraints is a praiseworthy achievement. "We could have simply stamped out these large panel openings and left it at that, but instead we devoted a lot of time and care to styling them correctly." The design idiom has to be a successful dialog such as that between free-style and compulsory figure skating. When asked about the overlapping demands of technology and aesthetics, Lai replies: "Sometimes the solution smells of perfume, sometimes of gasoline!"

This is where Porsche's designers look for their success formula: in the brilliant combination of logic, engineering, sporting style and visual appeal. The side view of the Cayman bears this out immediately. Features of the new coupé line are the boldly curved roof, long wheelbase and the sharp downward slope at the rear and in the side windows, together ▸▸

SOUND THE SIGNAL TO ATTACK: When it comes to agility, the Cayman has the edge

CLOSE-UP: The rear end of the Cayman twitches its hips most attractively

01 Design

THE UPSWING IS WITH US: Teardrop-pattern side windows lure the gaze upwards

BRIGHT OUTLOOK: A big glazed area is a feature of the new coupé body

EXPRESSIVE: The front lights add character to the Cayman in profile

01 Design

with an upward sweep that starts in the body sill light line and is continued by the rear side air inlets. Many new ideas, in other words, that had to find their way into a consistent whole. "Not too many!" warns Pinky Lai. "For every new part we not only have to consider elegance and style but also the need to guarantee production quality."

The rear-end concept, with its large glass area embedded between two muscular shoulders, is a good example of how the consequences have to be taken into account. The interplay of concave and convex inspires Lai, who normally favors a moderate choice of words, to exclaim "Brutal!" It called for many hours of overtime in the design department: the body construction experts pointed out that the original designs would involve extra stamping operations – a risk that no-one would willingly take. The Weissach studio was therefore asked to revise its design and reduce the angle needed to remove the panels from the press. This problem took at least a month to solve. Lai: "Form follows function, but forming the panels has to be taken into account as well." 'Form' and 'forming', in other words, have to come together before an attractive product can be made.

The Cayman is an individualist that nevertheless retains Porsche's basic formal concepts, for instance the important 'acceleration of surfaces' principle. The designer explains: The way we make a transition from a tight radius to a larger one is used everywhere to add vigor to the appearance of our sports cars." On the Cayman, this acceleration process is not limited to the roof area but applied in three-dimensional form throughout. "Look how the window surfaces accelerate from front to rear!" Yes, we can see it and appreciate it, without understanding just how it's achieved. Satisfied, Pinky Lai nods his head: this is precisely what the designer's philosophies and fantasies are intended to achieve. To help us, he explains further: "There are no sharp angles or edges anywhere on the Cayman. We prefer organic curves and we've maintained this principle right through to the back." On this sports car there are no sudden breaks that could disturb the overall styling harmony.

Another challenge accepted in masterly fashion by the Cayman's designers was to avoid surface interruptions. This too had consequences in the production and aerodynamic areas. The vertical wall that avoids unwanted aerodynamic lift on a sports car has to be simulated: styling freedom is never permitted to clash with fundamental physical laws. The extending rear wing proved to satisfy every requirement: it creates the "wall of air" needed for reliable tire grip, but remains invisible when not needed. It also gives the Cayman additional visual emphasis.

With the entire process complete, the result is a design that is highly emotive but also fulfills its functions effectively. The Cayman is transport for people who like to drive a Porsche rapidly and safely, and also a vehicle for their dreams and sensations. The designers' task has been to give these feelings free rein on the road. ‹

FORMAL PERFECTION: Curved surfaces instead of hard lines and edges

HUNTER AND HUNTED: The smooth transition between visual and dynamic appeal

01 Design

POLE POSITION: Even the seat adjuster knob is a delight to use

THERE'S NO CATCH: Even coats travel in comfort

LEVER ACTION: The seat responds to logical finger movements

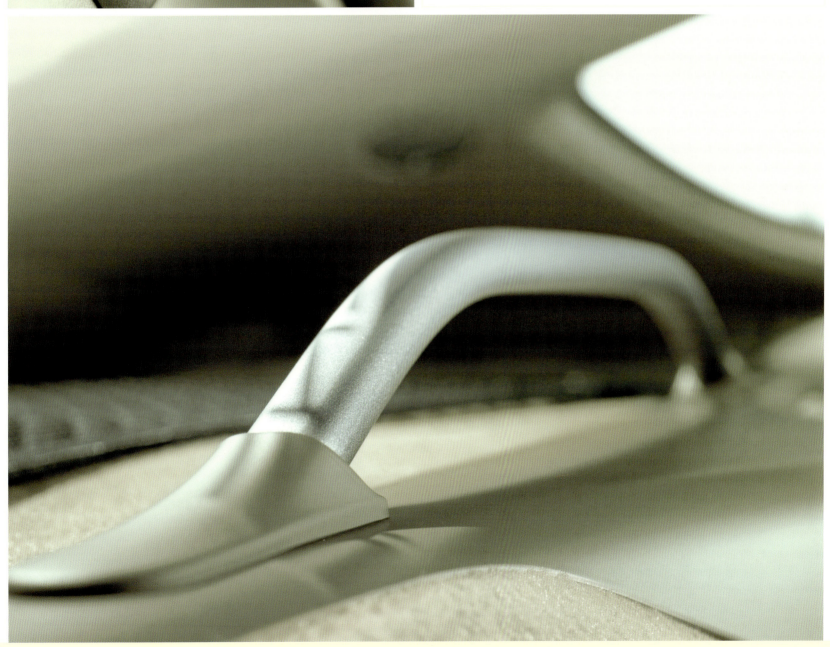

STOP: This hoop between the head restraints keeps luggage secure when you brake

01 Design

GRAB THAT HANDLE: A very positive feeling results when you open the door

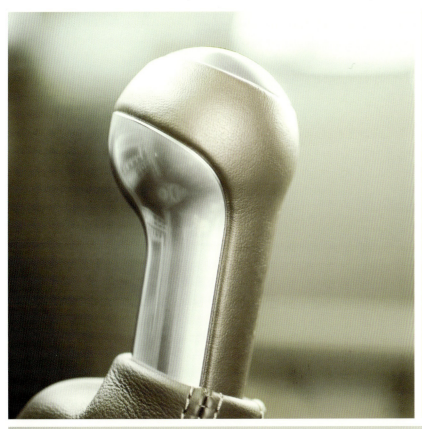

UP OR DOWN WITH FEELING: A gear shift it's always a pleasure to use

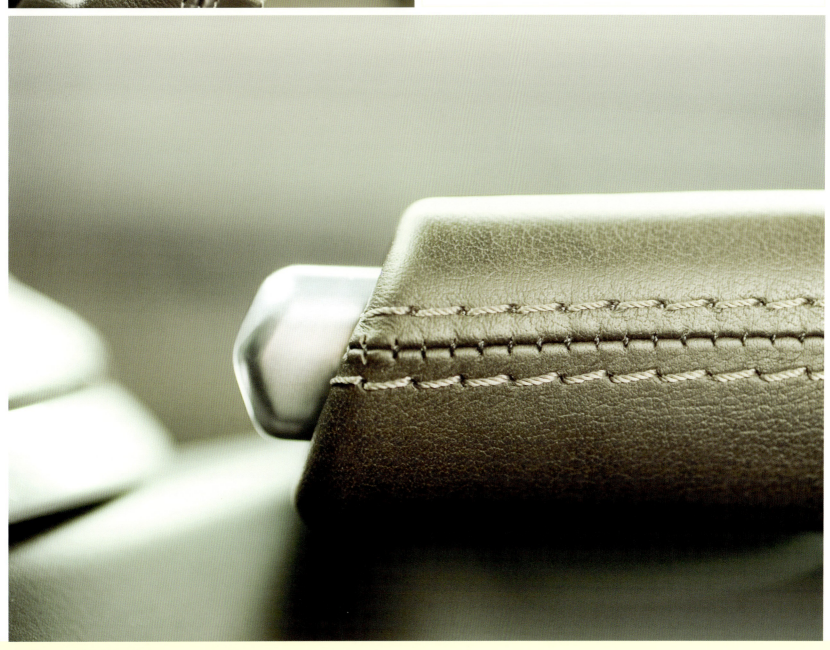

DOUBLE STITCHING: One handbrake lever, neatly and conveniently packed

01 Design

POACHERS AT LARGE

02 Body

PACK LEADER

The designers have taken to poaching from the material experts. It's their feeling for a good material mix that makes the Cayman the potent leader of the pack.

The very first glimpse of the Cayman from the front is a most welcome surprise. This free-flowing transition from the low windshield to the boldly curved roof recalls the integral visor of a safety helmet. Next, one sees the dynamic curve of the side sills, which the designers refer to affectionately as the 'ice hockey stick'. And then those opulently curved rear fenders! The Cayman is an iron fist in a most seductive glove.

To make such extreme sporty character visible from the earliest development phase on means knowing how to handle sheet metal and how to think in three dimensions – if three are enough! That's almost routine for Porsche's body wizards. But another of their tasks is to put the new car on a strict slimming diet. Weight is just unnecessary ballast for a sports car. Porsche cars are lightweights, but never at the expense of rigidity or passive safety. A contradiction in terms, one might say, but not for these artists in steel and aluminum. For them, it's a challenge that can be solved with modern materials and the latest welding techniques. A tough task, but a satisfying one.

Designers have a tendency to draw lines that simply can't be produced with the available materials and tools: a very good starting point for advanced thought processes. Nor must the need for a pleasant, adequately spacious interior be forgotten: the Cayman has it, and it's part of the car's own individual charm. Driver and passenger enjoy this feeling of space – a remarkable achievement in a car with the engine directly behind them.

Although the mid-engine is ideal for a two-seat sports car as far as its handling is concerned, few such cars have succeeded in communicating this sense of spacious, comfortable travel.

And the Cayman has even more to offer. The pack leader is generous to its occupants. The interior doesn't come to an abrupt halt just behind the head restraints; on the contrary, this is where the excitement starts. The rear trunk extends right back to the big window in the tailgate The side windows too have been lengthened: let there be light, a blessing that the occupants will appreciate.

To maintain this feeling, a few vital centimeters have been gained elsewhere too. The domed roof, with its sporty look, is very practical inside the car. Tall occupants in particular enjoy more headroom than they would expect in a car of this type. Space for long legs has also been provided: the firewall cross-member is made from ultra-high strength steel by a new method. This is of course mainly intended to increase the rigidity of the body still further, but it also optimizes the size of the footwells.

Having settled into one of these comfortable seats, take a long look backwards. The cockpit extends smoothly and attractively into the rear trunk. Since Porsche's engineers develop things together if they belong together, the trunk has been regarded as part of the car's interior on this model. Careful attention to detail can be seen everywhere: there ››

EMPHASIZING THE FIGURE: The curvaceous side panel is formed as a single piece

02 Body

are loops to secure loads and a neatly attached net to prevent them from sliding forward. The massive rear suspension struts are enclosed in elegant housings, but are prominently visible as a sign of the Cayman's authentic sports-car character.

The cover between the suspension strut domes is a brilliant design feature, and a sign that the stylists and body construction experts apply their minds jointly to such tasks. The first idea was to make it from aluminum and paint it in body color. The development team objected to this on the grounds that the paint finish would soon be scratched, for instance by opening the tailgate and dumping a bag or suitcase carelessly into the trunk. Sooner or later, this would have spoiled the appearance of the cover. Various materials were therefore tried out, the final choice being back-coated stainless steel – a special technique that makes the cover ideally strong and elegant. The effort may seem unnecessary at first, but the results are better in the end.

In addition to such ingenious problem-solving, the usual design tasks were performed on the Cayman with the determination and thoroughness for which Porsche is renowned. The front trunk lid, for example, is an aluminum shell element, weighing six kilograms less than if steel had been used. The tailgate with its heated rear window swings up to an extreme angle, and is of lightweight steel construction. The correct material mix is one of the secrets of Porsche's success, and complies with strict corporate policy rules: in every area of the car, the highest possible strength is to be achieved at the lowest possible weight.

Solving this material-mix puzzle has yielded a vehicle that's a sports car through and through. Naturally, the task isn't over when a lightweight material has been chosen for the trunk lid. The front and rear body side members, for example, since they determine the amount of impact energy absorption available in a frontal or rear-end crash, are made from what are known as 'tailored blanks'. These are produced by laser-welding precision steel sheets of various grades and thicknesses together. The aim is to guarantee optimum rigidity at precisely the points where it is needed, but at the same time avoid unnecessary weight.

A sports car has to stand up to severe treatment and resist forces acting on it from all directions. This even applies during the various production stages. The technical experts naturally attempt to comply with an almost irrefutable law of car body design, namely that the complete side panel should if possible be made in one piece. At first it seemed that the Cayman's side panels, with the gradual downward slope for tailgate location and the strongly curved fenders, would be impossible to make according to this principle. Such a 'difficult' shape, first convex, then concave, had not previously been attempted. The designers and body engineers fought over every centimeter – and finally arrived jointly at a solution that's brilliant and groundbreaking at one and the same time. The special fixture needed for shaping and cutting this complex side panel contains 180 metric tons of steel on each side, with six press tools each weighing 30 metric tons and exerting a force of 3000 tons on the sheet metal in the desired direction. Porsche's engineering teams can rightly claim that the Cayman is in top form ... ‹

HOOKS AND EYES: Loads can be lashed down firmly and are secured by a net

A SHINING EXAMPLE: Back-coated stainless steel is hard-wearing and also looks good

02 Body

DID YOU HEAR THAT?

03 Engine

LISTENING POST

Porsche? Sounds good! For the Cayman, the acoustics experts kept their ears pricked, their aim being to suit the mid-engine sound to the character of this new coupé.

The room is still, and occupied only by a complete Cayman car. Suddenly the silence is broken by a loud knocking noise. Nobody does anything as banal as shouting "Come in!" In any case, acoustics engineer Clemens Mutter is already there in the driving seat, performing one of the more straightforward tests that he and his colleagues employ: tapping various panels first with the knuckle of the left index finger, then banging harder with the whole hand.

More complex sonic techniques have already been applied during the Cayman's development: special engine test rigs, sensors and probes attached all over the car, an 'acoustic camera' and directional microphones. The aim is to reproduce and reveal precisely what the Cayman driver will hear later. The final test is Clemens Mutter's 'typical hand movement', which the latest Porsche has to endure whenever a series of tests has been completed. Porsche sports cars and their manufacturer have a high reputation to uphold. A final rap of the knuckles, and Mutter nods contentedly: the resonance is just as it should be.

The search for sonic perfection goes on at several levels. There is the sound the car's mid-engine makes. There are the noises that occur on the move, and those heard inside the car. Then there is the resonance that remains after its passage. A magic carpet of sound, but one woven in many ways. It obliges the acoustics team to adopt two entirely different approaches: one is boosting acceptable noise, the other is suppressing, or better still eliminating entirely, the less desirable noises. The quieter these can be made, the more evident the others will be. When the acoustics experts join the test-drive crew for the splendidly named 'Squeak and Rattle' trials, the radio stays switched off. The crew makes its own music, so to speak, which is why the interior of the Cayman looks like an operating theater engaged in some complicated heart surgery: sensors (as many as 390) are linked by a myriad of cables everywhere, including the trunk area. This acoustical spider's web is needed because noises are an ephemeral thing: identifying them is one thing, localizing them another.

Porsche's sound people don't rest until the proper acoustical balance has been found. This is a challenge, because although the Cayman itself generates the noise, various kinds of road surface act as a multiplier and have to be taken into account as well. The team was recently to be seen in a small African township, performing a routine that filled the inquisitive local population with amazement: a car with a dark paint finish accelerated toward the open country, braked hard after a few hundred meters, reversed and performed the whole operation again. The local residents gaped, and the acoustics specialists inside the car also had a surprised look on their faces, but for a different reason: a soft whirring »

CUE SOUND: It's the engine that makes the music in Porsche's acoustic measuring studio

EAVESDROPPER: The 'acoustic camera' localizes every sound

03 Engine

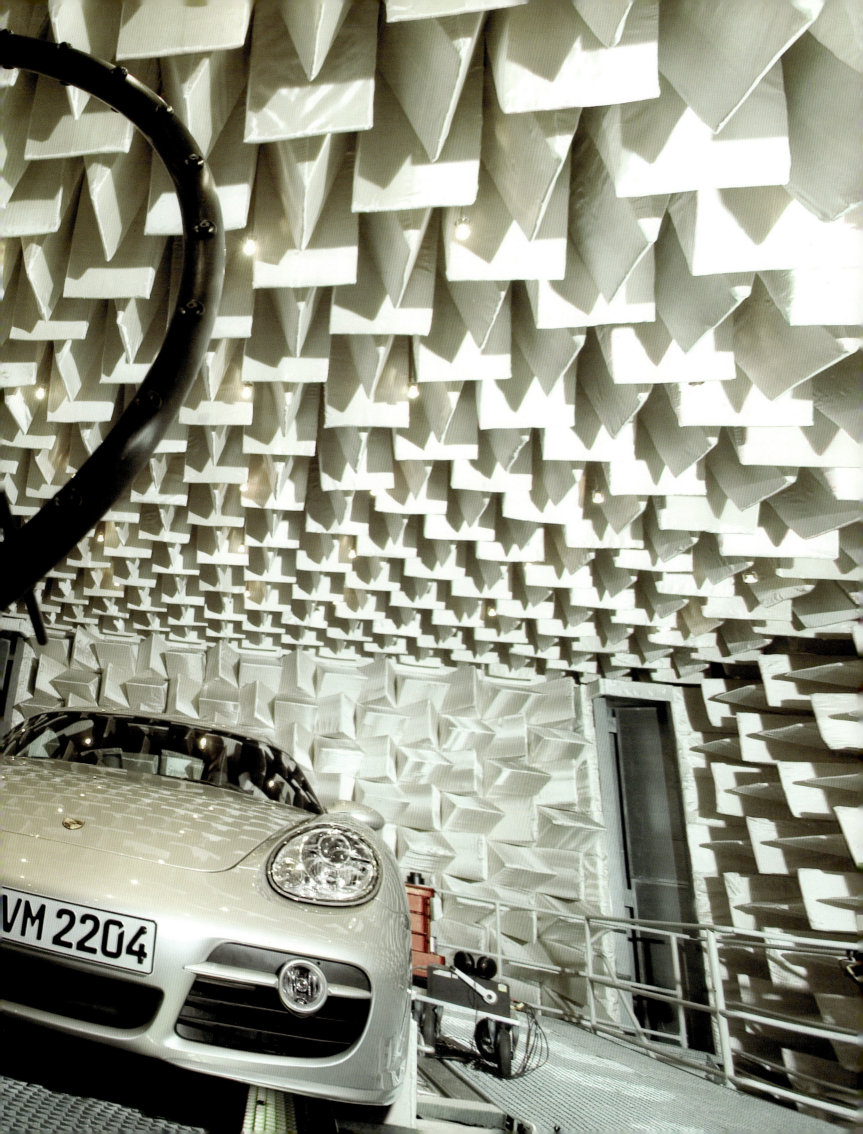

sound was audible, a sound of a kind that had not been detected on a single occasion during the preceding thousands of test kilometers. Could it be that the local asphalt road surface was generating a noise that had never occurred before anywhere in the world? How disastrous if one of the first owners of a new Cayman were to pass this way! Detective work was obviously needed. After repeating the acceleration test many, many times over, the team finally traced the culprit. The elegant cover concealing the oil and coolant fillers at the rear of the Cayman was causing this slight but none the less distinct noise. Isolating it with a strip of foam rubber provided a provisional cure, and the journey could continue. A similar heavy listening session tracked down a slight vibration in the tailgate, which led to the catch and lock being modified. Lengthy checklists are worked through during these road testing sessions. As we have implied, noises come in just two categories: those that irritate and those that please. A single noise in the former category is enough to spoil a most agreeable basic acoustic. It's best to listen to the acoustics wizards: what they hear is what we won't hear later.

The complete-vehicle acoustics department in Weissach employs about 50 qualified engineers to work on what we can safely define as the 'typical Porsche sound'. Their studios are an octagonal engine measuring booth and another for complete vehicles, both capable of achieving the highest standard of precision. The 'music' is mixed by Rolf von Sivers, who heads this department, and his team. It covers the full audible range, of which the powerful thrum from the engine is only one small part. In fact the higher frequencies are what give a Porsche its special sporty sound. To control the various frequencies is almost like rehearsing a symphony orchestra or, as von Sivers puts it, "perhaps more like listening to the musicians tuning their instruments. We vary the individual noise sources until we get a harmonious overall sound. Some of our 'soloists' need coaxing, some of them have to be threatened by waving the baton a bit more forcefully!"

This degree of subjective response is permitted, since it is a useful element in the objective search for the best possible sound. An overriding physical principle governs acoustic fine-tuning work on the Cayman: everything that could vibrate and generate unwanted noise has to be persuaded not to do so. On the positive side, the acoustics experts have a wide range of items that respond to tuning treatment in the engine compartment, including the valve gear, the crankcase, the air cleaner, the variable-length air intake pipe and the exhaust manifold. They know, however, that the human ear can be persuaded to hear only the more pleasant components in the noise pattern. The sounds that the Cayman's flat-six engine produces are healthy but never oppressive, >>

THE LISTENER: A dummy head simulates the driver and records noise inside the car

DATA TRANSFER: Special cables are needed to transmit data – even with the door closed

03 Engine

either inside or outside the car. Clemens Mutter, the man responsible for the 'good vibes': "The way a good sports car should sound!"

Vehicle acoustics are something of a hide-and-seek process. Every car has a number of 'acoustic bridges', for example the engine mounts, drive shafts, cables and hoses. They transmit vibration from the power train or the wheels. The driver senses this either as noise in the structure or as airborne noise reflected from the body. To minimize these effects, the acoustics engineers are consulted at an early stage, when the bodyshell is being designed. In the case of the Cayman, they asked for instance for the engine hood panel to be strengthened. The problem here was to avoid exceeding the weight limit specified for the complete car. Various materials were tested, listened to and reluctantly rejected. Finally, the choice fell on aluminum with angular reinforcements. A 'sound decision' ...

The Cayman's mid-engine coupé concept called for an entirely new, individual acoustic image. The aim was to strike a balance between low-frequency gas-flow noise and the high-frequencies generated by a fast-revving engine – without exceeding a tolerable overall volume of sound. A special 'mix' was needed, and led to a succession of acoustic tuning operations. Exhaust system components were cut out, narrowed down or otherwise modified, the audible response recorded, results compared and the mix modified yet again if necessary, until a typical Porsche sound that was also specific to the Cayman was obtained.

Everything the Cayman driver hears can also be seen in Porsche's acoustic measuring studio. Bright colored bars spread across the computer screens in the control center as the Cayman's engine note rises. An 'acoustic camera' supplies the data for this visual information. This is a far from straightforward concept: a video camera films the object generating the noise, and 36 microphones mounted on a frame locate the positions of the sound waves precisely. The audio and visual images are then superimposed, and the frequency ranges in which the sports car generates specific types of noise can then be seen. The camera takes no fewer than 19 200 snapshots every second, so that even the smallest sound is recorded reliably.

Does any driver give a second thought to the noise that's made by rain striking the roof of the car? The acoustics people in Weissach, with their sense of absolute pitch and tone quality, certainly do, and choose the insulating material for the roof lining accordingly. Since they have not yet found out how to stop it raining, they decided instead to re-orchestrate the 'Water Music' so that it's in perfect harmony with the Cayman. ‹

SOUND CHECK: Data are recorded inside the car and processed by computer

03 Engine

THE HUNT IS ON

The flat-six engines in Porsche sports cars are all members of a remarkably lively pack. Among them, the powerful 3.4-liter unit in the Cayman S goes its own way.

To be a Porsche engine is to be a member of a very dynamic family. Jürgen Kapfer, head of Cayman engine development, is obviously well aware of this. His comment: "The Cayman's flat-six engine is naturally related to the other Porsche engines, but it's none the less an entirely individual development." Almost all the main components are new: crankcase, cylinder heads, air intake system, crankshaft, main bearings and pistons. We're in the factory area where this engine was brought to maturity and where the finishing touches are now being made to the pre-production units. This is the experimental workshop in Weissach, and the Cayman's heart is getting ready to beat strongly. The aluminum crankcases are being moved from one workbench to the next on trolleys marked with the words 'Power Train'.

You can certainly sense the power among the people who work here. Jürgen Kapfer, as the responsible engineer, bends down to look closer at the components of one of the engines that are soon to disappear into the depths of the Cayman's centrally located engine compartment. The conrods in particular, and the production methods used for them, seem to impress him: "Forged and cracked – isn't that just remarkable!" The less well-informed onlooker is doubtful, and so a mechanic seizes the part in question and separates it with a special tool into the conrod itself and the big-end bearing cap. What looked as if it had been formed in one piece proves to be a broken-off section of the rod, the jagged edges of which fit perfectly together when the two halves are re-assembled and tightened. Conrods made by this method are stronger, and also happen to be unique, as one can see when the individual crack lines in the metal are examined under a microscope.

Engine development at Porsche is an exact science, and the relationships between the engine families often extend down to extremely small details. It's easy to imagine Jürgen Kapfer as a precision watchmaker. Terms like 'variable bucket tappets' make his eyes light up, and he handles the components in question like the finest table silver. Then he wipes a drop of oil off his fingers, an expression of quiet satisfaction on his face. Our compliments are politely declined. "Precision is part of the engine builder's craft", he says, "and here at Porsche a high degree of manual skill is part of the tradition."

The experimental engine workshop at the Development Center in Weissach is arranged in exactly the same way as the later production line in Stuttgart-Zuffenhausen. This is partly because the most efficient work sequences have to be established, but also to ensure a high degree of reproducibility, so that series production can subsequently go ahead without the slightest divergencies from the design specifications. The statement of sheer power that the six-cylinder engine makes would be altogether less valid if there were any unnecessary energy losses during its development.

It would be unfair to suggest that a new engine calls for strong nerves, but with up to 200 people engaged on its development, crucial mo- »

CONCEALED: The mid-engine is obviously happy in its hideaway behind the seats

03 Engine

ments do occur occasionally. The acid test, however, comes when the engine ceases to be a collection of individual components and is installed on the test rig for the first time. This is the moment of truth, known to the experts as "firing up". As the engine bursts into life, the onlookers are nervous: "Will it behave the way we expect it to?" The Cayman engine caused no trouble in this respect, though as Kapfer reminds us: "This is when the real work starts!"

A long road has to be traveled before the engine is cleared to run at 6250 revolutions a minute and develop its full output of 295 brake horsepower (217 kW), not to mention its peak torque of 340 Nm all the way from 4400 to 6000 rpm. Torque, the engine's secret treasure, gives the Cayman its superb pulling power and breathtaking acceleration. The basic concept matters too: mid-engined cars have always been noted for their dynamic handling and excellent traction, which naturally makes them ideal for two-seater sports cars.

The flat-six engine behind the seats may be the pacemaker that gives the Cayman its high pulse rate, but despite its many fine qualities it can't achieve everything on its own. It needs to be closely coordinated with its surroundings, that is to say not only the transmission in unit with the engine but many other assemblies as well. The engine management software has to be developed in parallel as vehicle applications vary. The engine is either adapted, or a point is reached where no compromises can be made. Fine tuning is often like walking a tightrope between such widely different values as fuel consumption, power output and emissions. To hide one's head in the sand could be to miss out on the optimized values for the entire package. Jürgen Kapfer is aware of this: "To develop a new vehicle with a new engine is a very exciting challenge!" He compares it to the work of the traditional shoemaker. "To have your shoes made to measure gives you a new walking experience. This 3.4-liter engine will always be identified with the car for which it was developed – the Cayman S."

Technical solutions have to fit perfectly too if the package is to be ideal. The engine developers have a firm principle: "The car's useable performance is not negotiable!" But in addition to sheer horsepower, the Cayman S has impressively high, uninterrupted pulling power at low and medium engine speeds, thanks to the adoption for the first time outside the 911 model line of the 'VarioCam Plus' camshaft and valve lift control system developed by Porsche. This engine is flexible and performs supremely well in city traffic and on country roads as well as at high speeds, thanks to inlet camshaft adjustment ('VarioCam') and a valve lift changeover system ('Plus'). The resulting 'two in one' concept has separate optimization values for idle speed and for part- and full-load operation, so that consumption and emission values also benefit.

It takes intelligent components and solutions like these to create a 'smart engine'. The intake air distribution pipe is a good example of this ingenuity. It is a double-flow unit with a switchable flap to generate additional torque at low engine speeds. The Cayman's agility, its freedom from vibration and its low center of gravity depend to a large extent on the unceasing flow of brilliant ideas that come from the active, flexible minds of its engine designers. ‹

SPORTY: An intelligent engine concept makes the Cayman S an intelligent sprinter

PULLING POWER: The Cayman S has plenty of it at low and medium engine speeds

03 Engine

FOLLOWING THE TRAIL

04 Road Dynamics

ON THE SCENT

Hurricane warning! The aerodynamicists in Weissach are hard at work tracking down excessive lift forces and high drag coefficients. The answer's in the wind!

In this long tube, the Cayman seems to be crouching ready to spring. The two-seater body looks capable of cleaving its way through the strongest of winds, and indeed this is what it is about to prove in the wind tunnel at Porsche's Aerodynamic Test Center in Weissach. The lights are as bright as those above a dentist's chair. Behind a slatted wall, three men are gazing alternately at their monitor screens and through the window at the sports car brilliantly illuminated in the giant tube below them. Graduate Engineer Thomas Aussem, disregarding the computer for the moment, asks: "Isn't it riding a few millimeters too high?" The reason is that the occupants are still missing. The driver, the passenger and their luggage are simulated by cans filled with sand that are dragged in from the preparatory workshop, and the car then has the right stance for testing to commence.

All the elements in the simulation must be correct from the start, or else the values will not stand comparison with the actual situation as it may be encountered later – and such comparisons are often needed. Being able to reproduce the results is just as important for ongoing aerodynamic development as accurate calibration of the wind tunnel itself. To ensure them even after several thousands of hours of operation, the soil on the entire site was filled with compacted material before wind-tunnel construction work began, and the foundations are supported on reinforced concrete piles that can be as much as 20 meters long. Such are the lengths, or rather depths, that are gone to in an effort to maintain the wind tunnel's accuracy.

The Cayman has to tolerate the same treatment as all other Porsche models before they are entrusted to the tender mercies of wind and weather. The eleven mighty fan blades of the 7.4-meter diameter propeller begin to turn. For the test being conducted at the moment, a wind velocity of 40 kilometers an hour is sufficient, but even then it is impossible to remain exposed to the wind in the 12-meter long test zone for more than a few minutes without wearing an anorak. And when the aerodynamicists genuinely stir up a storm, the wind whistles through at five to six times this speed. A complex pattern of blades, grids, coolers and honeycomb webs guides the airflow from this enormously powerful wind machine, which is rated at up to 2600 kW at 330 revolutions a minute. To explore the tunnel's geometry, the settling chamber, the broad-angle diffusor and the air nozzles is to feel oneself transplanted to a gigantic James Bond film set.

The wind is diverted at a right angle, and has to impinge on the intended target, whatever this may be, with great accuracy. Porsche's President and Chief Executive Officer Dr. Wendelin Wiedeking defied the airflow sitting comfortably on a chair, for a major daily newspaper's advertising photographs. The German four-man Olympic cycling team has been ›

CANAL WORKERS: A 7.4-meter diameter propeller puts the power into the airflow

04 Road Dynamics

LINES IN THE AIR: Smoke made by paraffin oil makes the airstream visible

STORM WARNING: The Cayman crouches low and defies the wind

04 Road Dynamics

checked for its aerodynamic efficiency here, and even a Black Forest cottage was stress-analyzed to make sure that the real thing would withstand winter storms. But it's more of a home match when the Cayman is put to the test. The airflow emerges from the 34-meter long diffusor and is accelerated to a speed of up to 60 meters a second at the outlet nozzle. This is when the 'tornado' phase of sports-car development begins.

To make the flow visible as it rushes past close (or not sufficiently close) to the Cayman's body, Thomas Aussem holds a lance in the airstream that emits smoke obtained by paraffin oil. The visible result can be compared to the jetstream from an airliner. To view these air patterns from the side is a most inspiring feeling. The whole procedure covering a new sports car's development period takes three years and six months, starting with a full-scale clay model. If the Cayman should find itself on the road in the middle of a hurricane, it would be essential to avoid aerodynamic lift in order to ensure reliable power transmission to the driven wheels. Yet the drag coefficient has to be kept as low as possible despite the demand for more cooling air for the powerful engine and brakes. Keeping a watchful eye on the drag coefficient is one of a sports car manufacturer's most important principles. A large frontal area, wide tires and, in the case of the Cayman, a relatively high roof line are all factors that make it extremely difficult to keep the drag coefficient low.

The aerodynamics experts therefore work closely together with the stylists until the smallest detail has been optimized.

None of the experts is prepared to rely entirely on know-how from the Computational Fluid Dynamics (CFD) programs, although these are already capable of illustrating the play of the winds around the car three-dimensionally. But this complex 3D technique is none the less an invaluable assistant, suggesting ways of working and preventing material from being consumed unnecessarily. Nevertheless, even the finest theory is all the better for having been confirmed in practice. Thomas Aussem comments: "In the wind tunnel we have made several discoveries that have improved the Cayman's aerodynamics and its appearance too. The test results tell us precisely where more development work is needed." One of the unceasing aims is to reduce aerodynamic lift: firstly to enhance the Cayman's sporty character, but also as a fundamental road safety factor. There is no value so good that it can't be improved upon, say the aerodynamics experts when they feel the urge to put the car through just one additional test.

Styling and aerodynamic requirements are brought into line step by step: the Cayman's front end is a good example of this. Together, the two teams worked on the basic shape, the panel curves and the radii until >>

WINDCHEATING: Plan view, body sweep and panel radii are all optimized in the wind tunnel

04 Road Dynamics

the airflow was optimized at every point. At the same time, satisfactory flows of cooling air to the high-performance engine and brakes were assured by efficient shaping of the side inlets. By careful design of the nose end, the sides of the front wheels were not only shielded against turbulence but air was also extracted efficiently from the wheel arches. Such tasks may seem a matter of course to the Porsche driver, but they 'raise the wind' in Weissach. Thomas Aussem: "A whole series of tests has to be run before the styling is finalized: if the technical development departments change anything, we run tests immediately." His serious expression seems to imply: zero tolerance is the order of the day.

Red digital numerals like an oversize alarm clock indicate the air speed in the wind tunnel. Human beings crouch down against the wind, but the Cayman retains its natural low-slung stance. The engineers watch the airflow patterns with something akin to affection. Is it fair to ask if they arouse 'aerotic' feelings? When the aerodynamics team members discuss the Cayman's appearance, they seem to look beneath the skin of its neatly styled body and recognize their handiwork. The A-posts, for instance, have a carefully chosen convex shape to keep drag and wind roar to a minimum even at high speeds and make the car even more of a pleasure to drive for long distances.

From nose to tail, this new Porsche coupé tells us what it promises the driver: tempestuous excitement. The downward sloping roof line and the tailgate have been just as effectively integrated into the overall aerodynamic concept as the rear wing, the exact contour and extension height of which were determined by an extensive series of tests, to make sure that it always operates in the correct aerodynamic zone for minimum rear-axle lift and drag. When Thomas Aussem and his colleagues set the mighty blades of the wind tunnel in motion, they probably murmur to themselves what Bob Dylan used to sing: 'The answer, my friend, is blowing in the wind.' ‹

IN A STATE OF FLUX: Efficient airflow over the roof, tailgate and wing

>>> 04 Road Dynamics

ON THE TRAIL OF DRIVING PLEASURE

Satisfaction calls for a perfect mix of all technical components. When the Cayman has finished a tough road test, not only the engine has to cool off.

The road surface must surely be at 60 degrees Celsius or more. But if the tires are hot, only the man at the wheel is to blame. He is a former racing driver and has transformed what was once a hobby into a second career as a test driver. His task today is to assess the suspension settings. He laughs contentedly as his right foot presses down on the gas and the car leaps forward. He says ominously: "Did you feel that? Now we'll enter the next corner deliberately on the wrong line. Keep calm!"

The passenger takes a deep breath. This is a close-to-the-limit experience – as indeed it's supposed to be. We can take the car for a relaxed run some other time. Today, it has to deliver all its power and show us the brilliant roadholding it's capable of. The test track in Weissach includes many an unexpected curve or hump. Full throttle here calls for genuine driving skill, and the awareness that the handling limits are very close indeed. This is Porsche's hunting ground, the ideal place to demonstrate the company's supreme chassis and suspension design skills and in fact its entire sports-car philosophy. With a skilled test driver at the wheel to take the car sensitively up to its handling limits, it is as if it were following the perfect line on an invisible set of rails.

The suspension copes effortlessly with all this severe treatment. On a sports car such as this, the stability control systems that provide driver assistance are designed to cut in late – so late, in fact, that even at high speeds a professional test driver has to make a deliberate mistake in order to stimulate these electronic helpers. This is why we are approaching the next bend on a totally incorrect line. "Did you notice how the stability system went into action?" the driver asks, "and how it kept the car on the correct path?" He accelerates out of the corner as if Michael Schumacher were just behind him. "Now I'll switch the system off!" The car hurtles through the hairpin bends, over sections of wet track, and the driver simulates avoiding action at well over 100 kilometers an hour. Then comes the slalom: an out-of-this-world experience. The car grips the road like a limpet, and if anything gets into a knot, it's only the unfortunate passenger's stomach.

"Terrific suspension!" says the man at the wheel. The North Loop of the Nürburgring racing circuit is over 20 kilometers long, and known to experts not without good reason as the "Green Hell". The Cayman S, with Sports Chrono Package, Porsche Active Suspension Management and 19-inch wheels, laps it in eight minutes, eleven seconds. Competitors struggle to match this, and even the 911 has to work hard to defend its lead.

Close behind the 911 on the road to ultimate driving pleasure, the Cayman is once again the 'Porsche Experience' in its purest form: confident and supreme in day-to-day driving, forceful and dynamic on the racetrack – an authentic sports car, no less. But the Zuffenhausen plant and the Weissach Development Center traditionally define their products by more than sheer engine power alone. Their recipe has mathematics, physics and subjective reactions as its ingredients. Or to put it another way, a magical mix of aerodynamics, weight-saving, power, suspension tuning and a sure feeling for the road.

Each Porsche model is given an ideal power train, in accordance with a systematic 'top-down' design principle: for the Cayenne, the company's off-road specialist that can carry the whole family in luxury, Porsche chose a front-mounted engine. The pure two-seaters, the Boxster and »

TIMED TRAVEL: The stopwatch on the dashboard is part of the Sports Chrono Package

CORNER-CRUNCHER: Lateral acceleration of more than nine meters a second

04 Road Dynamics

Cayman, have mid-engines and the classic 911, a 2+2-seater, derives its power from a rear engine. To satisfy even the most demanding standards of sports-car road behavior and maximum active safety, the suspension is also designed to suit the needs of each model line and matched to its performance.

Porsche uses electronic control systems only if they are of genuine benefit to the driver. This selective principle also helps to keep the car's weight down and make it even more fun to drive. Some of these systems are indispensable in the modern car, however, notably Porsche Stability Management (PSM). This communicates with the car's ABS (anti-lock braking system), ASR (wheelslip control), MSR (engine drag torque control) and ABD (automatic braking differential), and comes into action only when the car is likely to behave in a way that the driver cannot keep under control. Since a Porsche car is intended to assist the driver, not impose unnecessary restrictions on his or her actions, PSM is not over-sensitive in its response; for instance, it does not take effect too early at speeds below 70 km/h. The driver can switch the PSM system off, after which it only cuts in again automatically when ABS is actively regulating a front wheel brake application. In other words, this safety system is always available in the background and assists the driver when it is genuinely needed.

The Cayman driver enjoys even greater individual freedom with Porsche Active Suspension Management, which is available as an optional extra. The car's body rides ten millimeters lower when PASM is installed, and the shock absorbers have an active adjustment system. By pressing a button, the driver can choose between a sporty but comfortable ride (the 'Normal' setting) or a more emphatically sporty one that is also suitable for circuit racing (the 'Sport' setting). Within a few thousandths of a second the control system varies shock absorber firmness separately at each wheel on the basis of speed, lateral acceleration, vertical body movement and rates of braking and acceleration.

For drivers keen to check their lap times, the Cayman can be obtained with an optional-extra Sports Chrono Package. The stopwatch on the dashboard is a visual sign that a high-performance driver is at the wheel. But the package has other important functions too, including no-compromise control of the PASM, PSM and engine management systems. Shock-absorber damping force is increased and initial steering response is tautened for more effective road grip. The throttles open according to a steeper curve, engine response is even more rapid and the engine-speed governor cuts in later, though more spontaneously. The way in which these control systems influence the car's handling can be sampled on a circuit such as the Nürburgring's North Loop.

Drivers capable of maintaining such speeds must be able to rely utterly on the car's brakes. The Cayman's system is typical of a modern Porsche, with cross-drilled, ventilated disks and boldly styled four-piston monobloc aluminum callipers. It is ideal in terms of both weight and reliability. The brakes naturally had to pass the Porsche fading test, a murderous trial of any brake system, much feared within the automobile industry: the car is braked 25 times in succession from 247 km/h (90 percent of its top speed) to 100 km/h. Although this causes temperatures to rise as high as 700 degrees Celsius, they must not influence either the rate of retardation or the initial response. To achieve this, plentiful supplies of cooling »

TEST GEAR: Complex measuring devices record data during road testing

04 Road Dynamics

air are needed: they reach the brakes directly through apertures at the front of the body.

The latest tire generation, premiered on the new 911 in 2004, makes a major contribution to untroubled driving pleasure. The Cayman is shod with 235/40 ZR 18 front and 265/40 ZR 18 rear tires that have an asymmetric tread and use various rubber mixes for different tire sections in order to obtain maximum grip. 19-inch diameter wheels with 235/35 ZR 19 front and 265/35 ZR 19 rear tires are available as an optional extra.

Porsche has every technical facility at its disposal for suspension tuning, but human beings always have the last word. Thanks to the engineers' immense experience and the availability of advanced computer simulation methods, about 95 percent of what a car is capable of on the road can be determined at the design stage, but the last five percent, the 'fine tuning', has to take place on the road and involves considerable effort and expense. Some of the attributes of a true sports car such as a Porsche have to be finalized by driving it on the road. For instance, investigating the Cayman's behavior close to the handling limits took three weeks on the North Loop of the Nürburgring, with the car covering some 500 kilometers a day. Ride quality was tested on country roads and the German 'autobahn'. One of the most impressive results of this detailed development work on the Cayman S is the lateral acceleration limit of more than nine meters per second – the mark of a true cornering champion.

Such supreme road behavior is impressive enough in itself, but for true satisfaction the driver must also find the car pleasant to handle. The Cayman upholds its manufacturer's long tradition in this area: it maintains a continuous dialog with the driver so that no misunderstandings occur. Feedback from the accelerator and brake pedals and from the steering tell the driver reliably how the car is responding and how close it is to its performance and handling limits. Porsche pays especially close attention to brake pedal response. The motto in this case is 'constant force, constant travel', a highly emotional and therefore subjective situation that only an experienced engineer can assess correctly.

It is a memorable experience to sample the way that cars are driven on the Weissach test track. The driver hustles one last time through the slalom, then applies the brakes gently. "Well, you survived it!" he says, "but if you don't mind, I'd prefer you to stay where you are for the moment because we have to do one more cooling-down lap." He knows only too well that this applies to the passenger as well as to the car. ‹

MIND THE CONES: The slalom test demonstrates the Cayman's precision handling

TRADE MARK: Everything (or almost everything) revolves around the Porsche emblem

04 Road Dynamics

AN AGILE LIGHTWEIGHT

An athlete's diet aims for higher performance from less weight. Materials experts with the same approach tracked down every superfluous scrap of weight on the Cayman.

An embarrassed glance at the 'spare tire' around one's hips usually leads to the bathroom scales, where the sad truth is revealed. The higher the scale reading, the more depressed the mood. The opposite extreme is the obvious target: lower weight, more fun from life.

Porsche cars too benefit from this tough weight-saving diet. Their agility, dynamism and maneuverability come from having less weight to move around. This is why the definition of a Porsche doesn't just involve sheer power: low weight is just as important.

Porsche's engineers and material experts have a lot of experience of finding those excessive kilograms and eliminating them. It takes time and effort: after all, every single kilogram has a thousand grams. The calculation, however, is quite simple: a car that's 50 kilograms lighter can lap the notorious North Loop of Germany's Nürburgring circuit one and a half seconds faster. And the car's fuel consumption goes down too, by 0.1 of a liter per 100 kilometers.

The true quality of a sports car is expressed by its power-to-weight ratio – a simple calculation but one with pure driving pleasure as its result. The Cayman S is no exception to this rule. It weighs 1340 kilograms and has a power output of 295 bhp, which gives it a power-to-weight ratio of 4.5 kilograms per horsepower. Weight savings in the chassis and suspension area make a big contribution to this excellent figure. The front axle crossbeam, a pressure-cast aluminum component, is 30 percent lighter than if steel were to be used. The front and rear axles also make use of a complex, weight-optimized mix of steel and aluminum, with the components manufactured by various methods. Eliminating every scrap of excess weight has also led to the use of conical springs at the front, which are distinctly lighter than conventional coil springs.

Even the electronic control systems have to go on the same strict diet. The PSM control unit first used on the Series 996 version of the 911 now weighs three kilograms less than when it was introduced. Porsche's unbelievably systematic approach to weight reduction can also be seen in a basically unspectacular component such as the road-wheel carrier. This has been greatly modified in the past 17 years, since it now has much more severe loads to withstand – yet it has lost 5.4 kilograms in weight and is now 32 percent lighter at 3.7 kilograms.

Year after year, model for model, Porsche applies new yardsticks by lowering its self-imposed ideal weight limits. But don't worry: thanks to its brilliantly conceived aerodynamics, the Cayman won't take off! This comparison may help to convince you: the average jet airliner, weighing as much as 77 000 kilograms, leaves the runway at about 270 kilometers an hour. At the same speed, the Cayman is still exerting 1265 kilograms of downthrust – a triumphant application of day-to-day physical laws to ensure safe, enjoyable travel. ‹

IDEAL WEIGHT: Weight-saving design makes this sports car faster and more agile

04 Road Dynamics

WILD AND FREE

05 Experience

WHERE DANGER THREATENS

Freezing weather, driving snow, scalding heat, dust, torrential rain, deep water: test cars have a hard life in extreme climates. And sometimes a short one.

The search for isolation sometimes leads to unexpected surprises. A journey through barren desert scenery can be interrupted suddenly at any time. Somewhere in Africa, recent rainstorms may have failed to penetrate the bone-hard soil and diverted the course of a river across the road. Even the finest sports-car technology is powerless then. The car's occupants explore the new river bed on foot and sense its flow. In extreme situations the vehicles with generous ground clearance cross first and winch the sports cars over with their engines switched off.

Heinz Bernhard's term for what most of us would consider an exciting adventure is 'routine'. The cars and their occupants are back on the road, usually with no problems. But Bernhard has a tale or two to tell from his long experience of quality and endurance testing for the complete-vehicle development department. Not long ago, in the far north of Canada, the thermometer was, as so often, registering about minus 30 degrees Celsius. Early in the morning, a young couple had slid off the icy road in the middle of nowhere and plunged into a snowdrift. Panic-stricken, the driver struggled to extract the car, but only succeeded in flooding and stalling the engine, whereupon the heater wouldn't work either. The Porsche convoy happened past in the nick of time. The marooned couple was already exhibiting signs of frostbite and was grateful for the Porsche team's first aid. Bernhard: "We thawed them out strictly according to the instructions in the medical textbooks."

Travelers have tales to tell – and their accumulated experience is invaluable. This experience is what matters when Porsche dispatches people and machinery all over the world for road trials. This simple-sounding task involves covering several million miles, usually in the toughest imaginable conditions. Outside temperatures can vary all the way from minus 40 to plus 40 degrees Celsius, and all the most unpleasant aspects of the world's climate are likely to manifest themselves, from driving snow to a hot sun beating mercilessly down directly overhead, from torrential rainfall to sudden, violent gusts of wind. These journeys in search of extreme climates take the cars to the far north of Europe, the hot south-west regions of the USA or as far as the African continent. Icy roads, frozen lakes and dusty desert tracks are among the sought-after delicacies that the day-to-day driver would willingly do without.

Let us praise what makes us tough! Or to put it rather more modestly, let's face up to the inevitable. Porsche devotes a lot of thought to its 'adventure tours'. At the Weissach Development Center there are test rigs and low-and high-temperature climatic test chambers in which cars can have more hardships thrown at them than Mother Nature ever dreamed up – or are likely to occur in day-to-day driving. This is all well and good, but as in every aspect of daily life, practice is usually better than theory. At every stage of a new car's development – in other words three to four times in succession – it is flogged mercilessly for a distance equivalent to halfway around the world, all within a few weeks and including exposure to the most extreme heat and cold. The engine has to start readily and the engine operate reliably at unbelievably low temperatures. Every other technical feature has to perform equally well. Apart from sheer endurance, the car's handling and road behavior are thoroughly checked. These road trials answer the vital remaining questions that guarantee the customer true driving pleasure and satisfaction with his or her new Porsche. For instance, is the interior dustproof even if a strong wind blows across the desert? Is the steering wheel adjuster still easy to use the fifth time you try it? How hot does it get inside the car in strong, direct sunlight – and do unpleasant odors then occur? Does the sound from the »

EYES WIDE OPEN, VISION ZERO: Blind approaches are often unavoidable

ICE AND HEAT: At forty degrees below zero it's a chore, not fun

>>>> 05 Experience

exhaust not only motivate the driver at eight in the morning, but still strike him or her as acceptable after six hours of hard driving? Is there a road surface anywhere in the world that generates truly unbearable noise patterns inside the car? And so on – new questions are constantly arising.

As many drivers as possible therefore have to cover the longest possible distances in as many different cars as can be made available. Under test, a Porsche's entire roadgoing life or even more is compressed into an amazingly short period, and all this takes place in conditions more severe than any car sold to a customer would normally encounter. The testers at Porsche have calculated that one of their sports cars has to endure more during the test phase than a car used on the road for 30 years.

The test cars are treated most unfairly after undergoing such hardships. Porsche's internal rules forbid their being used subsequently for more normal purposes. Their lives are dramatic, but also short. In the experimental departments they are used for crash tests or to try out modifications. Within two years, the knell tolls. Heinz Bernhard: "They're usually so out of date technically by then that we can't use them for further development work." A sad ending for these heroes of tropical heat and eternal ice: they are disposed of quietly and efficiently by the proper environmental protection procedures.

The caravan moves on, and the next round of testing falls due. This time it may well be the turn of the Cayman. Its adventures start well before it is publicly announced, and therefore it has to be disguised. In the midst of the car convoy, this was relatively easy to achieve, to the extent that passers-by seldom identified it as something special. It would never do for cars to be identified as new models long before series production was due to start. Porsche therefore takes a variety of different models on each 'torture tour', to carry staff, spare parts and tools, measuring gear and iron rations. The team includes experts from various technical areas such as body, power train and suspension, but also a trained medical attendant with the necessary basic equipment, mainly for the treatment of colds and stomach disorders. The cars work hard, their drivers too. Including journey breaks, the convoy is usually on the move for between ten and twelve hours every day. The results are then discussed over an evening meal, during which some controversial opinions are often expressed. This shows the importance of subjective reactions to the car. If agreement can't be reached, decisions concerning modifications are postponed until the next morning. Road testing isn't just romantic adventure – it's a very serious business. To confirm this, Porsche's top management maintains a tradition of visiting the road test team to learn what conclusions it has reached.

The test routes are chosen very carefully. The aim is for the cars to be confronted with every kind of actual driving situation. Another important precaution before driving off into uncharted regions in the Cayman is to make sure that fuel is available about every 200 kilometers. On one occasion, the temperature dropped to minus 55 degrees in Alaska. The pumps were frozen solid, and some of the cars had to be left behind with enough gas for the engine to idle and keep the heater running, while the others searched for more fuel. After driving for an hour, fortunately, they found some.

A road test team recently returned from Africa with a more amusing story. In the middle of no man's land, they found a filling station manned by an obvious car freak, who identified their vehicles immediately as Porsches. After filling every tank to the brim, he shut up shop without more ado, declaring that he had now earned enough for a short vacation! ‹

CLOSE TO THE LIMIT: The test convoy is on the road for up to twelve hours a day

LOOKING BACK: A single test program simulates 30 years of typical driving

05 Experience

RENDEZVOUS IN THE SAND: Old love lies deep, but alas, time doesn't stand still ...

TEAMWORK IN THE HEAT: Checking, consultation, exchanging data, deciding what's best

HAND IN HAND: The drivers' subjective opinions are confirmed by advanced measuring equipment

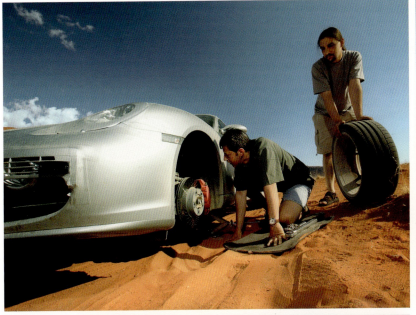

LOCAL CALL: Development Director Wolfgang Dürheimer (right) and Product Line Manager Hans-Jürgen Wöhler

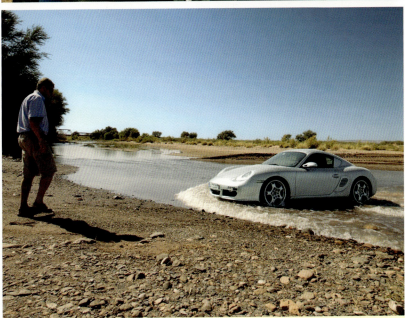

05 Experience

RUN THE PUMPS: Unexpected business for this isolated filling station

FILL UP, PLEASE: As a precaution, the team plans fuel stops every 200 kilometers

THE DESERT LIVES: But it's a tough test for power train, suspension and body

IN SHORT SUPPLY: A shady spot for a rest is a rarity

05 Experience

SPECIAL STAGE: Sandy tracks have never resulted in any severe problem

MAKING GOOD PROGRESS: The test routes include every conceivable kind of road surface

TRIAL OF STRENGTH: The Cayman S showed no signs of fatigue in the desert heat

TOWARD THE HORIZON: The Cayman test team disregards the weather

05 Experience

HAVE A BREAK: Time to analyze one's impressions of the preceding stage

STOPOVER: Members of the test team had to take their turn for refreshments here

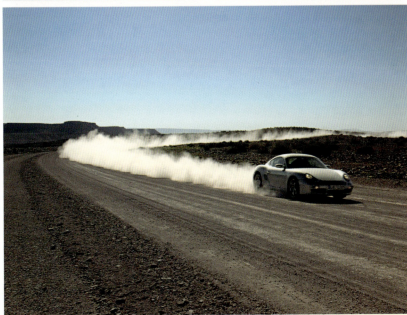

A TIGHT SHIP: Is the car dustproof? This is also tested in No Man's Land

TRACING TRADITION

Systematic weight-saving, maneuverability and mid-engined power: The Cayman's predecessor competed successfully in many motor racing series. It was the legendary Porsche 904.

What kind of fantastic things are happening in the middle of this bare factory building? We've made a flashback to 1963, and we're in Porsche's body construction department – though it looks more like Halloween at the moment! Resting on two wooden trestles – no, it's not an oversize pumpkin but a rather more elegant object: a sports-car body with the light gleaming on its ivory-colored panels. A closer look shows us what's in progress: the car's frame can be seen through the bodywork, a transparent vision, a gleaming example of perfection in automobile design: the Porsche 904.

When it was first conceived, this elegant creation was the ultimate interpretation of lightweight automobile design. The glass-fiber reinforced plastic body, for instance, weighed scarcely 100 kilograms, and was almost transparent before painting. From our standpoint today the 904, which was called the Carrera GTS in the first sales brochure, is an obvious precursor of the Cayman. Forget the advanced plastic body, transparent or not: the entire design is surely the way a two-seat sport coupe ought to be. Ferdinand Alexander Porsche – nicknamed affectionately "Butzi" by his family – produced drawings of quite remarkable, timeless vigor for the new competition car, expressing all its speed and agility and totally convincing to the eye at the very first glance. The 904 was built in accordance with these drawings, and is so low-slung that it could be driven under the axles of a big road tanker. This was promptly verified in the yard of Porsche's #1 plant!

The head of Porsche's museum, Klaus Bischof, has pictures of the illuminated 904 body carefully stored in his archives, but the relevant information is right there in his subconscious mind too. Ask him "What's the connection between the 904 and the Cayman?" and his inner eye lights up, so to speak. The answer comes immediately: "Look at the body outlines and you can see the 904 heritage. The classic concept of a two-seat sport coupe with mid-engine is ideal for a modern interpretation, and systematic weight-saving gives you a car with outstandingly good roadholding." Take a closer look at the two models, and the parallels become increasingly obvious, starting with the lights and air inlets at the front, through the neatly curved cockpit to the muscular wheel arches and the long, downward-sloping tail.

The 'Cayman of the Sixties' was born during a period of upheaval, both at Porsche and in motor sport generally. The company's original 356 model was gradually going out of production, and both customers and designers felt the urge for something new – which was to appear not long after as the 911. The competition department had just finished work on the Formula 1 project, and the new policy was to race series production cars. However, from 1964 on the rules in the Gran Turismo category, in which the young Porsche brand had already begun to make a name for itself, called for at least 100 cars to be built before a competition version could be licensed. "Butzi" Porsche took himself off to the drawing board and begin work on a new design. The 904 was a successful link between the 718 RSK Spyder and the 917. It is still regarded as one of the most attractive competition cars ever, and for many collectors it is the most elegant sport coupe of its day. Not only the 904's styling was ahead of its time: so was the engine intended to power it. However, the flat-six unit for which space was provided in the downward sloping tail did not appear in the 904 until later. The well-proven four-cylinder engine was adopted at first. The hundred or so cars with bodies built at the Heinkel aircraft plant in Speyer may have seemed rather modest compared with the company's series-production output, but in motor-sport terms this was quite a ▶▶

LIGHTWEIGHT DESIGN MADE VISIBLE: The 904's plastic body illuminated here from inside

PREMIERE SPLENDOR: The first 904, built in 1963

RALLY SUCESS: Böhringer/Wütherich were second in the 1965 Monte Carlo Rally

FLAT AS A FLOUNDER: The 904 passes the 'tanker test'

05 Experience

large batch of cars, and the private entrants' teams were overjoyed. The 904 confirmed the existence of a virtue deeply rooted in the genes of this sports car manufacturer: a latent desire for maximum efficiency. In the case of the 904, this meant discarding the competition car's customary multi-tube frame and aluminum panels for the much less usual plastic body concept. The selling price of 29,700 Deutschmarks for this ravishing road car with its clearly defined motor racing attributes could otherwise never have been maintained.

And indeed the 904 was soon at home on the circuits where motor racing history is made: Daytona, Sebring, Spa-Francorchamps, the Nürburg Ring, Le Mans. In 1964, its debut season, it satisfied Porsche's wish for an overall win against the overwhelming Ferrari and Ford competition. Only five months after the car's first appearance on the Solitude road racing circuit outside Stuttgart, Colin Davis/Antonio Pucci and Herbert Linge/Gianni Balzarini scored a fantastic one-two victory in the 48th Targa Florio, the legendary but extremely arduous road race on the island of Sicily. At the end of the first season, in the final race in Montlhéry, when the factory-entered cars were powered by the 210-bhp six-cylinder engine from the Type 901 for the first time, Porsche carried off the world championship title in the GT category up to 2000 cc, and was runner-up in the long-distance rankings and also successful in the Classic Challenge.

If there had been a trophy for many-sided ability, the Porsche 904 would have been predestined to win it. Very few cars in motor racing history, for instance, enjoyed success during their careers with a four-, a six- and an eight-cylinder engine. The private motor sport enthusiasts worshiped it as a true all-rounder. The 904 was seen on high-speed circuits, where its power output of 180 bhp at 7200/min gave it a top speed of up to 263 kilometers an hour, but also took part competitively in classic rally events, airfield races and hillclimbs. For the latter, a developed version with 'Spyder' body was produced as the Type 906. The 904 collected prototype, GT and other class wins in vast quantities. The list of leading racing drivers who took the wheel for the works team or one of the many customer teams is a long one, and includes such illustrious names as Edgar Barth, Dan Gurney, Gerhard Mitter, Jochen Rindt, Jo Siffert, Rolf Stommelen and Joakim Bonnier.

The Monte Carlo Rally, the yardstick for the performance potential and workmanship of all near-series sports cars, was chosen in 1965 to demonstrate the 904's qualities. Eugen Böhringer, better known as a Mercedes works team driver, and Rolf Wütherich, on furlough from his regular job as a competition department mechanic, enjoyed what was surely their most dramatic and memorable motor sport experience in the Maritime Alps. The much-feared "night of the long knives" was held in extremely poor weather, and proved to be little more than a hectic sleigh ride in deep snow. At the end of this rally, in which the brand-new 911 also took part for the first time, Böhringer and his navigator crossed the line as runners-up and assured themselves of a much-deserved place on the rallying scroll of honor and in Porsche's own history.

The 904, of which so many unusual stories could be told and which has been driven by many a prominent personality, achieved royal status in the course of its career when King Hussein of Jordan competed successfully in a number of rallies in his home country, at the wheel of a 904 with body number 008. Later he decided to exchange this car for a Carrera 6, and 008 was flown back to Stuttgart in 1975 in a Jordanian Air Force aircraft.

Since then, this 'blue-blooded' 904 has been cared for by the Porsche Museum, the ideal place to study the evolution of the brand and its models. Here one can clearly see that the Boxster is the legitimate successor to the 550 and, in the same spirit, the Cayman to the 904. One can also detect a design approach that remains valid even after forty years have elapsed: Porsche has never seen any reason why an attractive sports car should not be a successful one as well. To coin a phrase, "Beauty and the Bite" is a fair description of these cars! ‹

POWER PACK: The 904 Carrera GTS Coupe has a two-liter, four-cylinder engine

05 Experience

TWIN PIPES: Bold tail-end styling with visual evidence of a potent exhaust system

CLOSE RELATIVES: Like the 904, the Cayman has separate front-end lights

LET THERE BE LIGHT: The 904's tail lamps are simple, circular and convincing

05 Experience

RETRO-VISION: The 904's outside mirrors are elegant and sporty

ATTENTION TO DETAIL: The front hood lock (left) and side window opening (right)

UNDER LOCK AND KEY: The 904's fuel filler cap (left) and door lock (right)

05 Experience

THE HUNTING INSTINCT

06 Communication

THIS WAY!

Porsche's marketing and communication experts have, by coming up with a wealth of new ideas, given shape to the Cayman's public image.

Zero hour on the island of Malta: the sun obligingly broke through the rain-clouds and the thermometer climbed to an acceptable 20 degrees Celsius. Off Comino, the water sparkled in that clear blue that Hollywood film directors value so highly. This is where Brooke Shields swam through the 'Blue Lagoon' in her early nymphet days. But now it's March 2005, and a different but no less shapely figure is calling for our attention.

The Cayman is ready for its first encounter with this picturesque island, and for its first meeting with the people that represent Porsche on the world's markets. 160 importers and sales managers accepted an invitation from Head of Marketing Gerd Mäuser to fly to Malta directly after visiting the Geneva Motor Show. Porsche's President and Chief Executive Officer Dr. Wendelin Wiedeking, Sales Director Hans Riedel, Development Director Wolfgang Dürheimer and Head of Design Michael Mauer acted as a high-powered source of new-model information. The teams whose job it would soon be to introduce this new Porsche to customers around the globe set out for Comino in four sailing yachts. As they anchored, fountains soared out of the water like an official salute. What looked like a stone wall collapsed in response to a hidden signal – and there it was, the new Cayman S. Sun and water cast fascinating reflections on the body of the new coupé.

It's 'no holds barred' for Porsche whenever a new model is launched. Competitors in Germany alone spend hundreds of millions a year on advertising and public relations, whereas Porsche has only a small fraction of this sum at its disposal. Porsche's Head of PR, Anton Hunger, shrugs his shoulders: "Communication pressure is building up all the time, so it's our job to come up with something new!" PR and marketing experts work determinedly and creatively toward the company's long-term success. Their paths differ, but they have a common goal: to strengthen the brand's excellent image and stimulate interest in and admiration of each successive Porsche model.

Marketing tackles the task with these principles in mind. When a new model is under development, one question arises at a very early stage: what shall we call our new baby? Finding a name is an extremely complicated process that calls for legal minds as well as inventive ones. A new Porsche's name has to satisfy a variety of demands: it must be suitable for protection on the international market, which sometimes leads to lengthy research and negotiations with third parties. There's no time to lose: the patent offices are busy too. Worldwide, several hundred thousand names have already been registered in product category 12 ('Vehicles and devices for land, sea and air transport').

As well as these legal requirements, Porsche has its own preferences. The name must reflect the car's personality accurately and stimulate the correct response in terms of exclusivity, style and sporting character. As an inscription on the car, it must conform with the pattern established by the other Porsche model lines, and above all, people all over the world should be able to pronounce it without difficulty. For 'Cayman', tests were conducted over a period of 15 months before it was decided that this name was right for a sports car that's as thrustful, agile and dynamic as the eponymous baby crocodile.

Having chosen the name, Porsche established initial contact with potential customers via the Internet and by means of direct marketing »

PREVIEW: The Cayman S is the object of considerable curiosity

GOING ASHORE: 160 importers and sales managers on the way to Malta

06 Communication

END OF THE YELLOW PHASE: The Cayman attracts an enthusiastic crowd

MAGIC IN BLUE: Wendelin Wiedeking is obviously pleased with the new Porsche

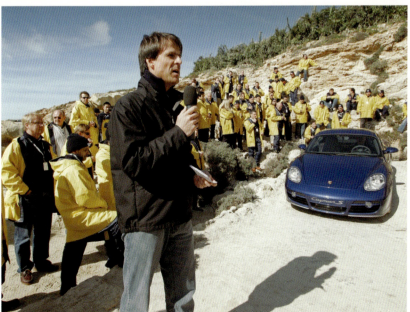

TELLING ALL: Head of Design Michael Mauer describes the practical features

06 Communication

IN THE WEB WORLDWIDE: The Cayman S joined the model line-up on the Internet very early

FULL THROTTLE: There's nothing better than trying it out for yourself

IN GOOD STANDING: Technical workshop for car journalists in Weissach

06 Communication

methods. The four-stage launch campaign is called 'Instantly Porsche'. More than 500 000 mailing shots were dispatched, containing increasingly detailed information, high-quality pictures and exciting film material on the new sports car. The response rate was even higher than the communication experts had anticipated, despite the fact that most of Porsche's contact addresses come from its own database and consist of people who have shown interest and have therefore been classed as potential buyers.

Early contact with the general public is very important, even before the first pictures of a new model are published. The first Cayman S advertisement didn't have a picture of the new sports car, just a photo taken in the twilight of three genuine caymans lurking in the water. The caption: "Hates corrals. Hates muzzles. Suits you perfectly. The Cayman S is coming. Instantly Porsche."

In the meantime, the public relations staff were planning the Cayman S market launch with the thoroughness of a military operation. When the first ad appeared at the end of February 2005, only the car's name and a few brief items of information on the new mid-engined coupé's performance and handling were supplied to the press. Three months later, Porsche mailed the first official photographs of the Cayman S to the media's editorial offices . As with previous Porsche models, these so-called 'teaser photos' served their purpose by getting the Cayman S onto the title pages of international car magazines without delay. In the best corporate tradition, the accompanying information was brief and factual. Anton Hunger justifies Porsche's purist approach in this respect as follows: "It's not up to us to say what great cars Porsche builds. Our task is to give the journalists all the important facts so that they can decide for themselves how good the cars are – and how good they look!" For the first time, Porsche offered leading international photographers a week's opportunity to portray the Cayman S in their chosen style in the studio, before the world premiere.

To emphasize its leading position in modern sports-car development, Porsche regularly holds technical workshops for car journalists. The Cayman S launch was an ideal opportunity to invite more than 130 representatives of the international media to a four-day event at the Development Center in Weissach, and explain effectively how, for example, the suspension control systems work, how the car's weight has been kept down and what the latest braking system can do. In this way Porsche creates a sound basis for greater public interest, and this was satisfied on a grand scale at Germany's International Motor Show, held in Frankfurt in September 2005, when the Cayman S was premiered in front of a enthusiastic public that was immediately captivated by the appeal of this rebellious 'baby crocodile'.

Immediately afterwards, at the information event for the international Porsche dealer organization, it was once again 'Instantly Porsche'. When the cruise liner 'Seven Seas Voyager' reached the port of Ibiza late in the evening, the 1600 dealers were looking forward to a presentation of the new model the next morning. But the Cayman had a few more surprises in store for them: fireworks, fountains of water as high as the buildings, artificial fog and a laser show accompanied the first burst of sound from the mid-engines as eight Cayman S cars converged on a steel ramp several meters high, built on the quayside wall. A perfect backdrop for the new sport coupé: high above the port of Ibiza with a view of the island's twisting roads as a reminder of tomorrow's driving.

At the driving event held at the same time in Tuscany, the international press had a chance to drive the Cayman S on specially selected roads. The market launch in November 2005 was the final stage in the new model's communication strategy. Together, Marketing and PR had achieved their goal of a successful launch.

Now the Cayman S is free to roam – and for customers to take it to their hearts. ‹

Hates corrals.
Hates muzzles.
Suits you perfectly.

The Cayman S is coming.
Instantly Porsche.

POISED TO SPRING: The task of the first Cayman S
advertisement was to arouse curiosity

06 Communication

CAYMAN S – TECHNICAL DATA

The easiest way to familiarize yourself with the inner values of the Cayman S is to take a closer look at these facts, figures and brief technical descriptions.

BODY
Two-seat coupe, load-bearing bodyshell of optimized lightweight construction using sheet steel galvanized on both sides; full-size front, side (thorax) and head airbags for driver and passenger

AERODYNAMICS
Drag coefficient	$C_d = 0.29$	
Frontal area	$A = 1.98$ m²	$C_d \times A = 0.57$

ENGINE
Water-cooled 6-cylinder (flat six) with aluminium engine block and cylinder heads; 4 valves per cylinder; variable valve timing (VarioCam Plus), hydraulic valve clearance adjustment, variable-length intake pipe, integral dry sump lubrication, two starting and two main catalytic converters, 4 oxygen sensors (lambda probes) with stereo control system; engine oil content 9.7 liters, cooling system content 22.3 liters; DME (Digital Motor Electronics) managetment system for ignition, fuel injection and camshaft adjustment; electronic ignition with solid-state distributor (six separate coils); sequential multipoint fuel injection

Bore	96 mm
Stroke	78 mm
Displacement	3,386 cm³
Compression ratio	11.1:1
Power output	217 kW (295 bhp) at 6250/min
Max. torque	340 Nm at 4400 – 6000/min
Output per liter	64.1 kW
Max. engine speed	7300/min
Fuel grade	Super Plus (RON/MON 98/88) unleaded
Electrical system	12 Volt, 2100 W, alternator, battery capacity 70 Ah

TRANSMISSION
Engine and gearbox bolted together to form a single unit; rear wheels driven by double universal-jointed halfshafts

Ratios	Manual	Tiptronic S
1st	3.31	3.66
2nd	1.95	2.00
3rd	1.41	1.41
4th	1.13	1.00
5th	0.97	0.74
6th	0.82	–
Reverse	3.00	4.10
Final drive ratio	3.88	4.16
Clutch diameter	240 mm	

SUSPENSION
McPherson struts at front and rear (Porsche-optimized), independent suspension using trailing arms, conical coil springs surrounding twin-tube gas-filled shock absorbers ››

FULL FRONTAL: A low frontal area means good aerodynamics

SIDESIGHT: Powerful progress is where the Cayman S excels

BRAKES
Dual circuits (one per axle), 4-piston monobloc aluminum calipers; ventilated brake discs, diameter x thickness 318 x 28 mm at front, 299 x 24 mm at rear; PSM 8.0, vacuum brake servo

WHEELS AND TIRES
front	8 J x 18, 235/40 ZR 18
rear	9 J x 18, 265/40 ZR 18

WEIGHTS
Unladen weight (DIN)	1340 kg
Gross weight limit	1630 kg
Roof load	60 kg

DIMENSIONS
Length	4341 mm
Width	1801 mm
Height	1305 mm
Wheelbase	2415 mm
Track	
front	1486 mm
rear	1528 mm

Luggage capacity acc. to VDA test method   410 liters (total)
Fuel tank capacity   64 liters

PERFORMANCE*
Top speed	275 km/h (267 km/h)		
Acceleration	0 – 100 km/h in sec.	5.4	(6.1)
	0 – 160 km/h in sec.	11.7	(13.5)
	0 – 200 km/h in sec.	18.6	(21.6)
	0 – 1.000 m in sec.	24.3	(25.4)

FUEL CONSUMPTION*
acc. to EU standard	urban	15.3	(16.3) liters
per 100 km	extra-urban	7.8	(7.9) liters
	total	10.6	(11.0) liters

CO_2 EMISSIONS*
acc. to EU standard   254 (262) g/km

* Values in brackets refer to cars with Tiptronic S transmission.

ALL ALONG THE LINE: The Cayman S combines performance potential with supreme design

PUBLISHER'S DATA

This edition published in 2006 by Motorbooks, an imprint of MBI Publishing Company, Galtier Plaza, Suite 200, 380 Jackson Street, St. Paul, MN 55101-3885 USA

© Dr. Ing. h.c. F. Porsche AG, 2006

ISBN-13: 978-0-7603-2581-0
ISBN-10: 0-7603-2581-2

Printed in China

Previously Published by	Dr. Ing. h.c. F. Porsche AG, Public Affairs and Press, Anton Hunger
Editors	Christian Dau, Sabine Schröder
Texts	Jutta Deiss, Elmar Brümmer, Reiner Schloz
English Translation	CB Übersetzungen GmbH, Munich
Design	Atelier Machart, Stuttgart: Valerija Wolf, Bettina Scherrieble, Anke Koblinger
Blocks	immedia23, Stuttgart

All rights reserved. Rights to the utilization of illustrations and text contributions are held by Dr. Ing. h.c. F. Porsche AG, Stuttgart, and reproduction, transfer to other media or copying either wholly or in part are prohibited unless express permission has been granted.

PICTURE CREDITS	Page
Christoph Bauer	74/75, 80/81, 82/83, 86/87, 98/99, 138/139 (lower pictures), 105 (bottom left picture)
Markus Leser	18/19, 44/45 (upper pictures), 46/47, 50/51, 52/53, 54/55, 56/57, 60/61, 62/63, 64/65, 66/67, 68/69, 76/77, 78/79, 85 (upper picture), 124/125, 128/129, 130/131, 132/133, 134/135, 136/137, 139 (upper picture)
Stefan Warter	8/9, 12/13, 14/15, 16/17, 22/23, 26/27, 28/29, 30/31, 32/33, 34/35, 36/37, 38/39, 40/41, 42/43, 44/45 (lower pictures), 48/49, 58/59, 70/71, 72/73, 85 (lower picture), 88/89, 90/91, 92/93, 142/143, 144/145, 146/147, 148/149, 150/151, jacket
Ingo Barenschee	96/97, 100/101, 102/103, 104/105, 106/107, 108/109, 110/111, 112/113, 114/115, 116/117, 118/119
Porsche Archives	120/121, 122/123, 126/127
Premium Picture Agency	6/7, 10/11